A Family in South Korea

This edition published 1987 by Lerner Publications Company. All U.S.
rights reserved. No part of this book may be reproduced or transmitted
in any form or by any means, electronic or mechanical, including
photocopying and recording, or by any information storage or retrieval
system, without permission in writing from the publisher, except for
the inclusion of brief quotations in an acknowledged review. © 1986
by Gwynneth Ashby. First published by A & C Black (Publishers)
Limited, London, under the title *Korean Village*. Map on pages 4-5 is by
Tony Garrett. The photographs on pages 8 and 19 are by Man Su Hong.

LIBRARY OF CONGRESS CATALOGING-IN-PUBLICATION DATA

Ashby, Gwynneth Margaret.
  A family in South Korea.

  Summary: Describes the busy life of eleven-year-old Chun Yung
Mee who lives with her family in a village in the Republic of Korea.
    1. Korea (South)—Social life and customs—Juvenile literature.
2. Family—Korea (South)—Juvenile literature. [1. Family—Korea
(South) 2. Korea (South)—Social life and customs] I. Title.
DS904.A83 1987   951.9'5   87-3478
ISBN 0-8225-1675-6 (lib. bdg.)

Manufactured in the United States of America

  2   3   4   5   6   7   8   9   10   97   96   95   94   93   92   91   90   89

A Family in South Korea

Gwynneth Ashby

Lerner Publications Company · Minneapolis

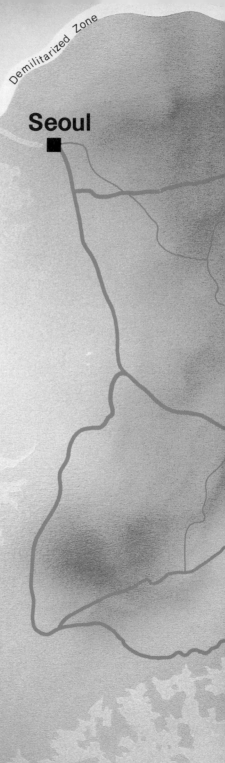

Seoul

This is Chun Yung Mee. She's the one in the red dress, playing her recorder with a friend. Chun is her family name so most people call her Yung Mee. She is eleven years old and lives in Ochun (oh-chun), which is a village in the Republic of Korea. It's about 120 miles (200 kilometers) from Seoul (soul), the capital city.

CHINA

USSR

Sea of Japan

JAPAN

NORTH KOREA

Demilitarized Zone

SOUTH KOREA

Yellow Sea

4

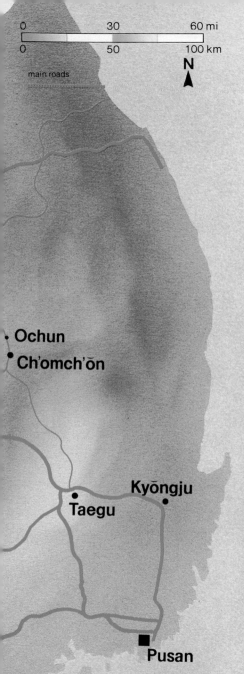

0 30 60 mi
0 50 100 km

main roads

N

Ochun
Ch'omch'ōn

Kyōngju
Taegu
Pusan

Korea is divided into two countries: the Republic of Korea, which is usually called South Korea, and the Democratic People's Republic of Korea, which is usually called North Korea. Yung Mee's grandmother remembers when the North Koreans crossed the border and fought with the South Koreans. The war started in 1950 and lasted for three years. The border is still closed between the two countries and it is difficult for people to cross over to visit friends and relatives. Yung Mee and her family and friends are sad that Korea is divided.

Most of Korea is covered by mountains. Yung Mee can see mountains from her house. The fields below them are where people from Ochun grow rice.

5

There are seven people in Yung Mee's house: Yung Mee and her sister Yung Hee, her two brothers Yung Il and Yung Hoh, her father and mother, and her grandmother. All the brothers and sisters of a family usually have the same middle name.

Yung Mee gets along best with her sister, and they sleep in the same room. Here Yung Mee is making her bed. The mattress and quilt are kept in a closet, and at night she takes them out and unrolls them on the floor. It's very warm in winter because the floor is heated by pipes from the kitchen stove. The family uses the stove to cook on as well as to keep the house warm.

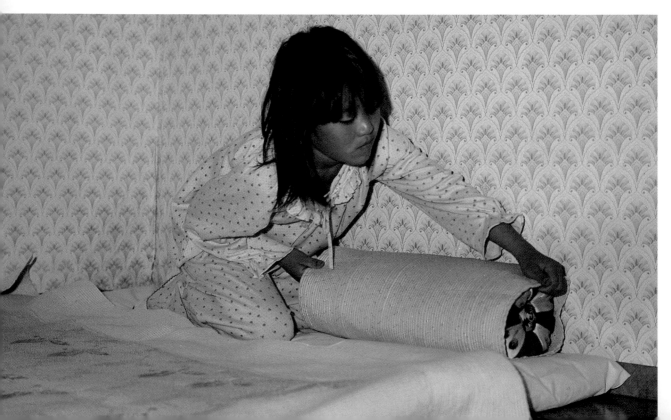

This is the front of Yung Mee's house. Everyone uses the verandah, especially in the summer. It's shady there even when it's too hot and sticky to play outside. Grandmother likes to sit there when she's preparing vegetables.

The Chuns leave their shoes on the verandah. No one ever wears outdoor shoes inside the house.

Yung Mee's father has storehouses in the yard in front of the house and a stable for the cow and her calf. The family's well is in the yard too. At the moment the Chuns carry in their water, but soon they won't need to. There's a Korean group called *Saemaŭl Undong* (say-ma-uhl oon-dohng), which means New Community Movement. It gives each village help in becoming more modern. Mr. Chun and some neighbors have already widened the main street, and next they're going to lay water pipes. Then the Chuns will have a faucet in the kitchen.

Everyone eats dinner in the family room. They're having pumpkin soup, fish, and vegetables. There's always lots of rice for dinner—the Chuns eat eighteen bags a year. That's nearly 2,200 pounds (1,000 kilos).

Yung Mee's mother uses an electric cooker for the rice and does the rest of the cooking on the coal stove. She has a refrigerator-freezer, but they switch it on only in the summer because electricity is expensive. She says it costs too much to have the refrigerator on all year. She and Grandmother dry a lot of food for the winter. Yung Mee helps by picking persimmons and threading them on strings. When the whole persimmons are spread out in the sun, they turn sugary and taste wonderful.

The Chuns always have *kimch'i* (kim-chee) with their meals. It's a sort of pickle made out of a mixture of cabbage, radishes, garlic, and red peppers. Some kinds of kimch'i are spicier than others, but they're all quite hot.

In the summer, Yung Mee's mother makes kimch'i every week. In November she starts pickling vegetables to make winter kimch'i. She fills two large pots with the mixture and buries them in the ground. The kimch'i will keep fresh in the frozen earth so they have kimch'i until spring.

Mr. Chun has two jobs. He gets up very early in the morning to drive people to work at the coal mines near the village. Then he brings the bus back and starts work on the farm.

In the autumn, Mr. Chun spends most of his time harvesting rice. Then he loads the sacks of rice into his pickup truck and takes them to the Ochun mill.

In addition to rice, Mr. Chun grows crops like peanuts, soybeans, and sweet potatoes. The Chuns' pumpkins are some of the biggest in the village. Yung Hoh can hardly carry them.

On weekends, Yung Mee sometimes helps in the orchard.
The Chuns start picking apples in July and don't finish
until the end of October. The whole family helps to load
the pickup. They grow five kinds of apples, but Yung Mee
likes Golden Delicious best. After they've taken the apples
home, Mr. Chun packs them into wooden boxes and puts
them in the storehouse.

Mr. Chun and Grandmother built the storehouse last
year. Now they can keep apples until January or February,
when they can get more money for them. Some of the
Chuns' apples go to Seoul and other towns in Korea, and
some are sent as far away as Japan and Hong Kong.

There aren't enough jobs for everyone in Ochun, and some people don't want to work in the country, so they move to the towns.

Yung Mee's friend's sister, Kim Wol Tai, moved to Seoul. She works there in a silk factory. She's in charge of four looms which weave silk thread into cloth. When they run out of silk, she puts in new bobbins with more thread.

The flag for the 1988 Olympic Games was made at Wol Tai's factory. The silk all came from cocoons spun by silkworms in Korean villages. It takes hundreds of cocoons to make a piece of silk.

Yung Mee watched for the flag from Wol Tai's factory flying in the Olympic stadium during the Games in Seoul. Yung Mee had seen pictures of Seoul on TV before the Olympics. It always looks enormous and very busy to her. The streets are jammed with traffic and there are hundreds of skyscrapers. Wol Tai has told her about riding on the subway, and she'd really like to try that.

Most of all, Yung Mee wants to see the Olympic Stadium in person. She watched the opening ceremony for the stadium on TV in 1987. In 1988, she watched as much of the Olympic Games as her parents would let her. It was exciting to have people from all over the world visiting her country for the Games.

It only takes Yung Mee five minutes to walk to school, so most days she leaves home at 8:00 A.M. She tries to get to school early so that she can do some extra work with her friends before class starts. Her class has some important tests next year and they'll all have to work hard to pass them.

Class goes on all morning except for a short break, and at 1:00 they go into the playground to eat the lunches they've brought. Yung Hee goes home at lunchtime because she isn't old enough for afternoon school. Yung Mee's little brother, Yung Il, doesn't go to school yet. He'll start next year when he's seven.

Yung Mee and her big brother, Yung Hoh, bring lunchboxes and chopsticks to school. Their mother packs lunches of cold rice and snacks like sausages and hard-boiled eggs. Sometimes they get *kim pap* (kim-pop), which are made of crispy seaweed filled with rice and vegetables, rolled up and cut into slices. After lunch, they play until lessons start again.

When school is over, they have to clean the classrooms. They all wash the floors and take turns to clean the windows and the toilets and to pick up the playground.

After that they can do what they like until the teacher goes to take down the national flag. As it is lowered, they salute the flag. They salute the flag before school, too, when it is raised. They're very proud of their country and their flag.

This year, Yung Mee's class went on a trip to Kyŏngju (kyawng-joo). On the morning of the trip, she was so excited that she got up much too early. Her class went on a special school bus and it took them more than two hours to get there.

When they arrived in Kyŏngju, they wanted to look in the stores, but their teacher said they had come to see the sights, not to shop.

The first place they went to was Tombs Park. The dead kings and queens of Korea are buried there, but all you can see are big mounds of grass. The class went inside one of the tombs, called the Tomb of the Heavenly Horse. There used to be crowns and jewels inside, but now there are just copies, so the teacher took them to see the real ones in a museum. Yung Mee really liked some gold earrings with green pieces of jade.

Then the class went to Pulguk (bool-gook) Temple. At the gates of the temple there are four huge statues. They're the kings who guard the temple. Behind the railings in the picture you can see devils being squashed under the feet of two statues. The students had to walk all the way up a mountainside to see an enormous Buddha statue. Their teacher said that it was more than a thousand years old and that they should be proud of it because it's so old and famous.

On the way back most of the class fell asleep on the bus. Yung Mee did too. The next day everyone had to write a report about what they saw and did on their trip.

When Yung Mee gets home from school, she usually watches TV or rides her bike. Yung Hoh has a new bike, but the girls have to share one. In the evenings they all do lots of homework. Mr. Chun has bought a set of encyclopedias because he wants the children to do well at school, but Yung Mee says they're too hard for her. Maybe the encyclopedias will be more useful when she's older.

On Wednesday evenings she goes to a club where she's learning English. This is her name and the name of her village in *hangūl* (han-guhl), which is the Korean alphabet, and in English.

Chun Yung Mee

전 영 미

Ochun

오 천

Yung Hoh stays after school to play baseball. In the evenings when Yung Mee is doing her homework, Yung Hoh sometimes practices *t'aekwŏndo* (tay-kwon-doh). This is the martial art of fighting with hands and feet. Yung Hoh says it keeps him fit.

School closes in December because it costs too much to heat the classrooms in the winter. The students have home-work assignments every day until school starts again in February, but there's still time to play.

Most Sundays, Yung Hoh and his friends have to get up at 6:00 A.M. to clean the village. The Saemaŭl leader tells the boys what needs to be done. Yung Mee is glad she can stay in bed.

Every September, Yung Mee's school enters a school band and dance competition. The Ochun school band is one of the best in the area. Lots of Yung Mee's friends play in the band. Rehearsals are very noisy and lots of fun.

The girls in Yung Mee's class do the Fan Dance. They dress up in traditional Korean clothes called *hanbok* (hahn-boke) and put flower crowns in their hair. The dance is very graceful. They all dance in groups, moving around each other and making patterns with their fans. The dance gets faster and faster, and at the end they make a huge circle, snap their fans open, and wave them up and down.

The boys have a dance, too, called the Battle of the Wagons. It's between two teams, the East and the West, and it's very noisy. The boys use two poles as the wagons, and at the top of each pole there's a boy who's called the *cox*. Everybody wants to have a turn as cox and wear the special costume.

The other boys stand at the bottom of the poles and steer them while the cox shouts orders—"Right!", "Left!", "Forward!" The winning team is the one that knocks the other cox off his pole. If the East team wins, the village will have a good harvest. But if the West wins, the crops will fail. At least that's what people used to believe. Yung Mee says that now it's just a game.

There are a few food stores in the village, but when Yung Mee's mother wants to buy clothes she shops in Ch'omch'ŏn (chom-chawn). It takes only half an hour to get there by bus. Ch'omch'ŏn has a market and when the Chuns' calf is old enough, Mr. Chun will take it there to be sold.

In October the stalls in the market are loaded with the things that go into winter kimch'i—cabbages and radishes, and huge bunches of onions and garlic.

The Chuns don't buy vegetables at the market because they grow all of theirs at home. Yung Mee's mother usually goes to the market for clothes and useful things for the house, like rubber gloves. Yung Il gets tired and rather bad-tempered walking around the shops and street markets. Sometimes his mother buys him a toy to keep him happy, but if she has a lot of shopping to do, she picks him up and gives him a piggyback ride.

Yung Hee really likes going to Ch'omch'ŏn. She keeps trying to get her mother to buy her a ball. Yung Mee would rather have a hot cake from one of the stalls there.

23

The Chuns are Buddhists. In one of their rooms they have an altar in memory of Yung Mee's great-grandmother. They leave gifts like dried fish and apples on it to respect her memory.

They also follow the teachings of Confucius, who lived in China thousands of years ago. One of the things he taught is that children should be polite and helpful to their parents, their teachers, and especially to the elderly. On buses, Korean children always give up their seats to old people. If Yung Mee meets a teacher out of school, she bobs her head to show respect.

At harvest time, there is a thanksgiving festival called *Ch'usŏk* (choo-sock), when everyone tidies their ancestors' graves and leaves gifts for them. Everybody in the village celebrates. The Chuns' next-door neighbors go to a party held by some friends from the church Sunday school.

Yung Mee likes Ch'usŏk. It's a time when her relatives visit from the town and they have lots of presents and special food. Halfmoon rice cakes are her favorites. They're pink or white or green, and you don't know what's inside until you bite them. It could be raisins or pinenuts or sugary red beans. At Ch'usŏk they wear their hanbok clothes and play games. Yung Mee is playing jacks in the picture.

Mr. Chun takes the family camping every summer. They load tents into the back of the pickup and go off to a little town in the mountains. Only Grandmother stays at home to look after the animals.

Last fall, during school vacation, Yung Mee went to Taegu (tay-goo) with Nam Sook Hwa, who lives next door, to visit some friends. It took more than two hours to get to Taegu by express bus from Ch'omch'ŏn. The bus hostess told everyone to fasten their seatbelts, and then she put on a tape so they could listen to music. Once Yung Mee went on an express bus which even had TV.

Yung Mee and Sook Hwa knew they were getting near to Taegu when they could see factory chimneys from the freeway. Taegu is the third biggest city in the country and it has lots of huge buildings.

Sook Hwa's friends live in a modern apartment building. By the apartments there's a playground and a swimming pool. When Yung Mee was there it was too cold for swimming, so they played on the slides and merry-go-rounds, and bounced on the trampoline.

Yung Mee likes the wide streets in Taegu and the department stores and supermarkets. But she would rather live in her own village. It's quieter there and the air is cleaner, and she knows everybody.

The Korean War

The Korean War was part of the struggle between Communist and non-Communist countries, involving China, the Soviet Union, the United States, and other countries.

Korea was first divided when the Allies took it back from Japan at the end of World War II. The Soviet Union, which was one of the Allies, occupied the north. The United States occupied the south. Then the Soviets wouldn't leave.

In 1947, the United Nations (or UN), said that the Koreans should hold elections to choose one government for the entire country. The Soviet Union would not permit elections in North Korea, so each half set up its own government. Both North and South Korea claimed the entire country, and their troops fought several times.

In 1948, the Soviet Union said that it had removed all of its troops from the north. The United States then took all of its troops out of the south in 1949.

On June 25, 1950, North Korean Communists invaded South Korea. The UN demanded that they withdraw. The Communists kept fighting so the UN asked its member nations to help South Korea. Many UN countries sent troops, military equipment, or supplies to the South Koreans. The United States sent the most aid. The North Koreans received troops from China and military equipment from the Soviet Union.

Millions of people were killed, wounded, or left homeless by the war. The war ended on July 27, 1953, when North Korea and the UN signed a truce. North Korea and South Korea have never signed a peace treaty and American troops are still stationed in South Korea.

Facts about South Korea

Official Name: Republic of Korea

Capital: Seoul

Language: Korean

Form of Money: won

Area: 38,025 square miles (98,484 square kilometers) not including the demilitarized zone, a strip two and a half miles wide along the border between North and South Korea

> The United States has about 95 times the area of South Korea.

Population: About 42 million

> The United States has about six times the population of South Korea.

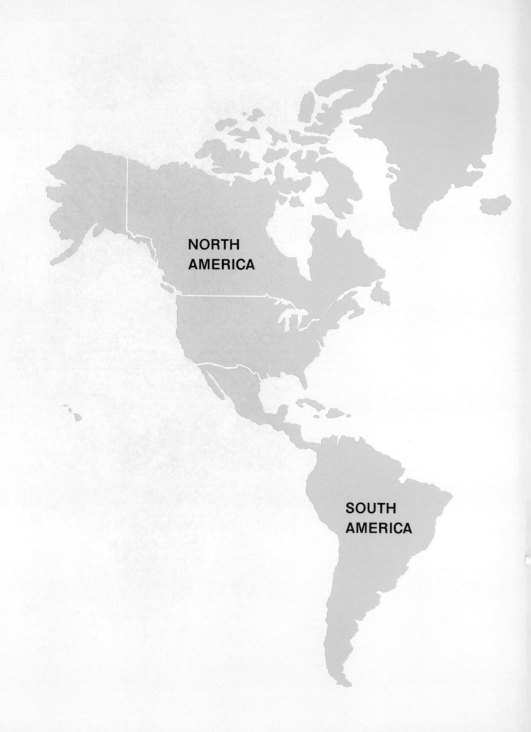

NORTH
AMERICA

SOUTH
AMERICA

EUROPE

A S I A

South Korea

AFRICA

AUSTRALIA

Families the World Over

Some children in foreign countries live like you do. Others live very differently. In these books, you can meet children from all over the world. You'll learn about their games and schools, their families and friends, and what it's like to grow up in a faraway land.

An Aboriginal Family
An Arab Family
A Family in Australia
A Family in Bolivia
A Family in Brazil
A Family in Chile
A Family in China
A Family in Egypt
A Family in England
An Eskimo Family
A Family in France

A Family in Hong Kong
A Family in Hungary
A Family in India
A Family in Ireland
A Kibbutz in Israel
A Family in Italy
A Family in Jamaica
A Family in Japan
A Family in Kenya
A Family in Liberia
A Family in Mexico
A Family in Morocco

A Family in Nigeria
A Family in Norway
A Family in Pakistan
A Family in Peru
A Family in Singapore
A Family in South Korea
A Family in Sri Lanka
A Family in Sudan
A Family in Thailand
A Family in West Germany
A Zulu Family

Lerner Publications Company, 241 First Avenue North, Minneapolis, Minnesota 55401